T0072305

Power Poetry
for the
Soul & Everything
in Between

Me, My Mind, My Journey

SHAMILA SAEED

authorHOUSE®

AuthorHouse™
1663 Liberty Drive
Bloomington, IN 47403
www.authorhouse.com
Phone: 833-262-8899

© 2023 Shamila Saeed. All rights reserved.

No part of this book may be reproduced, stored in a retrieval system, or transmitted by any means without the written permission of the author.

Published by AuthorHouse 08/09/2023

ISBN: 979-8-8230-1309-3 (sc)
ISBN: 979-8-8230-1310-9 (e)

Library of Congress Control Number: 2023914936

Print information available on the last page.

Any people depicted in stock imagery provided by Getty Images are models, and such images are being used for illustrative purposes only. Certain stock imagery © Getty Images.

This book is printed on acid-free paper.

Because of the dynamic nature of the Internet, any web addresses or links contained in this book may have changed since publication and may no longer be valid. The views expressed in this work are solely those of the author and do not necessarily reflect the views of the publisher, and the publisher hereby disclaims any responsibility for them.

Contents

Preface

I would love you to open this book with a cup of chai or coffee. And some cookies even because, why not? As you read this, you may pause and say, "I get this." This book is a mixture of poetry and thoughts written when reflecting on experiences or in a moment of enlightenment.

My hope is that you find something that resonates with an experience or thought and have that aha moment. If something makes you laugh or smile, great! My wish is that some words will be inspiring, moving, motivating, and helpful to you.

Acknowledgments

This book is a project that has been in pending mode for ages. I motivated myself a whole lot through the ups and downs of life to keep pushing. My sister, Rahila, has been a motivator pretty much my entire adult life, and my number one fan. Thank you, Rahi.

Thank you to the production and creativity team and everyone who worked on making this book a reality. To my family and fellow humans in my life who always believed in my goals, thank you. You know who you are.

And a big thank you to my mom and dad. I was raised by you the way you were raised, and I have moved forward, taking valuable lessons, and adding my spin to parenting and life. We are from different generations, but we learn so much from each other through our experiences. And the love we have for each other is priceless. I love you both. Thank you for believing in me.

Brown Skin

Brown is the color of my skin.
Some people may call me yellow-skinned.
Back home, some people will say my skin is too dark.
My brown skin is my skin and just right.
I like to stand out, not fit in.

B is for brave.
I endured so much pain.
At the hands of humans, I suffered.
Courage found me, always to do right by me.
Bravery did not lead to a loss for me but gain.

R is for resistance.
Anything harmful to another human being, I refuse to
    accept sitting.
Racial inequality, human inequality, anti-human rights
    politics—
We can be better than this as a human race.
We need to keep standing for equality and fight until
    we win.

O is for one.
There is only one me.
Unique, like every human being, but one together as a
    human race.
I once wanted to hide from the world.
I have come far in my journey and now want everyone
    to see me.

W is for woman.

Being a woman, I have a duty to raise other women up, to speak up, and stand up.

Being a woman is amazing as women are pillars of strength.

Do not listen if they say being a woman is just about physical beauty.

We are beautiful inside and out, and so much more.

N is for never.

Never give up.

Never let someone hurt you again while waiting for them to treat you better.

Never settle again.

Never question your worth again.

Never stop fighting for yourself and others.

Never stop using your voice. Be heard.

Never apologize for being you.

Never stop loving yourself.

Never stop loving your brown skin.

Home

Where every breeze brings in the scent of jasmine through
    my windows,
Where I can hear the rain and feel at peace.
Where the flower petals in the garden fall from old
    blooms,
And new buds flourish to life.
This is home.

Where the footsteps of a child make my heart sing,
And the warmth every afternoon sunshine brings.
Where bread is broken in harmony;
Where hearts of the young and old are whole and joyful.
This is home.

Where good memories are a reminder of goodness,
With every rainfall a blessing, washing away sorrow.
Every petal that falls is an old memory to cherish and
    remember,
For every fallen petal is a promise of new blooms, new
    memories.
This is home.

(In memory of my grandmother, Hamida.)

Island

The sea-green waters of the ocean shimmer,
The sun beating down so brightly.
The heat warming the calm water,
Freshness filling my soul as I step in.

The green, lush palm trees swaying in the breeze,
Dancing to the rhythm of the Caribbean beats playing
on the beach.
The pink, red, and yellow flowers so bright,
Their scent traveling down the shore.

Beautiful colors and sweet aroma of fruit tempt me,
Wanting to try every mango, coconut, guava.
The market and ocean breeze nearby drowning me,
Asking me to stay on this island.

Island life is calling me,
Melting away the hustle of mainland life.
The love and colors of the island call me,
Beckoning me to make this home.

(*Written in St. John, 2021.*)

Deafening Silence

The angry waves of the ocean fill my ears with noise,
Water crashing against the rocks.
The sounds of the ocean bring peace
To the broken soul in need of respite.
When there are no words,
Nothing is spoken by the one,
The one soul that makes your heart sing;
Hearing their voice has been music to your ears.
But nothing is heard,
Bringing all to an end.
And my voice catches in my throat
From the pain of understanding this.
The deafening silence envelops me,
An empty void left in me.
I walk by the screaming ocean
In hope of peace for my broken soul.
The angry waves crash into the rocks,
Chaotic yet silent.
Such is the turmoil in my heart.
What I hear is deafening silence
Where I hoped for peace.
A reminder of this pain.
The empty void tells me, reminds me,
They are lost to me.
I am lost to them.

The Eyes of a Daughter

Sometimes you must break your own heart
For the right reason.
My reason is my daughter.
She is the most important reason
To not accept anything less than what I deserve,
To value my worth,
And to be strong.
Her beautiful eyes watch me,
And she will exert the same value on her life
That I have to my own.
Find your reason to do right by you when it's hard.
You are worth it.
Your reason is worth it.
She is worth it.

A Plan for the Anxious Mind

We struggle having been hurt, yes.

When hurt, we shut down or become anxious,

And it's lovely when another human understands this and supports us.

Our anxious behaviors are either understood or deeply misunderstood.

With another understanding human, we must try.

We must do our part and try

To have calm and peace in our hearts,

And peace in our present relations.

Do not let past relationships

Control and hurt your present ones.

We are responsible for our own thoughts,

Not someone else.

We owe ourselves peace and healing.

We owe those who want to know us, love us, a chance.

For the sake of fairness,

For the sake of love,

Because we all deserve to be loved,

No matter what our struggles may be.

Do better, be better, feel better,

And trust the process of your journey.

Life

Appreciate the small things in life.
Appreciate the people who care,
The air we breathe,
The hands that pull us out of darkness.
Show appreciation today,
Not tomorrow.
Life is a temporary gift to the world.

Growing Old Reality Check

That moment when you google a handsome actor and learn you're old enough to be his mother.

Identity

This is not who I am.
I know exactly who I am,
And I am not changing.
You can only reveal the real me
When I feel safe and appreciated.
If I am not being right, being me,
Something is not right,
And something must change.
Just not me.

Abortion Bans in the United States, 2022

A woman will have to suffer bringing a pregnancy to term even if she could die, even in cases of rape. Worse, a child will have to suffer bringing a child into this world even if raped, even if she may die. Let that sink in.

Timing

A lot is happening for me right now.
I am grateful and blessed.
I do not say much,
But I notice many things.
It is fine if you don't clap for me.
Whatever prevents someone from being happy for another
Is likely something that consumes them.
You are better than that.
Your time will come when the timing is right.
I hope your time comes soon.

A Seat at the Table

Even if you have messed up,
God forgives you and has a seat for you.
Even if you feel inadequate,
He cherishes you
And has a seat for you.
Even if you're skeptical and doubtful,
God's love for you doesn't waver.
And your seat has your name assigned to it.
The choice to take it is yours.
What's important is that you forgive yourself first;
Learn to forgive yourself.
Taking a seat at the table is a choice as a human being,
And you are no less than anyone else on Earth.
No matter what table you choose to sit at,
Be kind to yourself, and be loved as you are.

Survival at Sunset

The sky breaks open over the water,
Bringing many colors into its depth.
You can find peace within its depth,
And let it empower you.
That same water can drown you.
Rise above it.

Personal and Professional Space

People are like very tight underwear. If you stretch them too thin, they wear out quickly.

The Power of Silence

Confidence is silent;
Insecurities are loud.
We have heard this saying,
Or at least heard that silence is golden.
Knowing this,
It is still difficult to keep quiet
When someone hurts us.
But we must power through it somehow
Because no words matter the most then.
And all the words in the world won't matter at all.
So practice silence,
Especially for your own peace of mind.
Happiness does exist
Outside of unfortunate events in life.
We just need to look harder.
Don't stop believing that.

Breaking Down Walls

Self-love and self-worth are keys to growth and happiness. These are your two most vital tools to break down any walls you have built up around your soul to keep love out. Empower yourself.

The L Word

There is a stigma around using the L word
If social norms are followed.
Break the social norms, and just say it.
Just be careful to whom you say it.

You can feel all the love for someone in the world,
But make sure they are worthy of receiving those words
    from your lips.
Saying I love you changes everything.
The brave will stay;
The deserters will go.
Why are people so afraid of love?
There are a million ways this question will be answered,
And no story will be precisely the same.

Sacrifices and Secrets

Your happiness with someone is not enough for other
     people,
Although it should be enough to see you happy.

Happiness is not meant to be contained and conditioned.
Happiness is unconditional joy,
Deserved by all and to be shared.
But we hide it away
For safekeeping, guarding it.
It will be ripped away if they knew.

Time goes by quickly when we're happy with someone.
But it feels frozen as well
When you are bound to hide joy
For the sake of keeping it.

The expectation is that we abide by what makes others
     happy.
We are told we will find happiness, be rewarded by doing
     as we're told.
They don't understand this is fake, conditioned happiness
     and love.
They don't understand they've asked us to suppress our
     dreams.
They don't understand they've asked us to limit our joy.
They just don't understand.

After the sacrifices are done,
And everyone has filled their cups with victory,
I find myself standing alone at square one,
With broken dreams and wishes.

Trying again is the tough part.
Going out of my way to be vulnerable,
That is the tough part.
To let my walls down again is frightening.

I have sacrificed valuable time.
It was the hard lesson I needed but undeserved,
To understand that my time must be respected,
Time that I can never have back.

Time cannot turn back,
Allow us to start over.
Only if that time was not taken,
My tired soul would have been more charged.
But I have some strong woman genes,
And I am still standing.
I still have some fight left in me.

A Women's World

Chivalry will not be dead when women are the only ones found on earth. We already hold doors open for each other.

Motherhood Pain and Pride

My most cherished memory:
Holding my baby for the first time.
The pain of bringing life to this world gone,
Replaced with pride so overwhelming, I cry.

Working to provide,
To show my baby hard work.
To show independence and strength,
To one day exert that same pride and forget pain.

Pain in this world is inevitable.
It's how we handle it and rise above it.
For my baby will see one day
Pride and joy chosen by us will always overshadow the
    pains of life.

We are not here by chance.
We have been given the gift of life.
We are sent to this world imperfectly perfect
To find appreciation of ourselves and others.
To be thankful for being here
To find purpose.

A mother knows that her child is like none other.
I am grateful that this baby was gifted to me.
If only my baby could see through my eyes
How rare and beautiful they are.
The world around this child will always be more colorful
For without my baby, my small world cannot be as bright.

Understanding a Tired Soul

How can I expect him to communicate with me if he struggles to understand me? There can be no communication if there is no comprehension.

Letting Go

This man has a strong hold on my heart. As painful as things get, overwhelming even, I cannot stop loving him. When you get to that unexpected threshold, you will try to hold on because that love is what is familiar. Keep pushing forward, and you will find your grounding and peace.

Self-Forgiveness

I forgive myself for staying silent,

Allowing others to think I am naïve.

I notice things and feel things so strongly and so well.

I forgive myself for not being blunt and upfront

For my silence is just to not rock the boat.

I forgive myself for putting others first,

Staying silent so not to cause stress,

But drowning myself in stress.

I forgive myself for dishonesty so to protect others from stress,

And drowning myself in guilt.

I forgive myself for putting so much energy into others

Without it being matched and draining myself.

I forgive myself for loving so deeply without returned affection.

I forgive myself for not understanding how to love who I love,

Even with so much love to give.

I forgive myself for being afraid of vulnerability.

I forgive others for not understanding how to love me,

Perhaps not wanting to understand me.

I forgive others for not asking if I was okay

When I was not okay.

I forgive myself for being too hard on myself.

I forgive others so I can forgive myself.

Reluctance

I do not say much in response to things I should not hear
or see,
But that does not mean I did not hear or see.
I take notice and keep moving with hope,
Hoping that things will turn out all right.
Giving folks the benefit of the doubt has a limit.
When that limit is breached, I reluctantly move away.
Reluctantly because it hurts.
Reluctantly because I expected more from that person.
The person I know, deep down inside,
The goodness is all there.
All of it.
Just not for me.

Self-Opinion

Self-righteous people are found everywhere. Don't let their assessment of you color your opinion of yourself.

Misuse

Women are resilient. However, taking a blow repeatedly is exhausting and damaging. Stop using our resilience to normalize mistreatment and disrespect.

Misunderstood

There is a certain way that some humans speak to me
That triggers two types of responses:
I shut down.
I respond, panicked.
Being spoken over will not elicit a good response from me.
Not being able to finish speaking will give space to
    misunderstand my half-spoken words.
Going into a panic and continuing to speak when I don't
    want to be heard will hurt me, not them.
Sometimes people are not as caring as you thought.
People can lose compassion and not even see that
People point out what's not right and disregard everything
    that is right.
People insult my commitment and capabilities.
People forget that I am human.
And maybe that is because I forget to give myself grace,
So why would others,
Even if I push myself to the limit in the most trying times
    of my life.

For Me

Like me,
Read with me,
Look at stars with me,
Teach me,
Walk with me,
Share your laughter,
Share sorrows,
Cry with me,
Tell me your secrets,
Trust me,
Love me,
Defend me,
Get mad at me,
Fight with me,
But always fight for me.

Dear Whoever Needs to Hear This

A woman's place is *not* in the kitchen. If you disagree, let's fight. I will bring my sandals and you bring your rolling pin.

Unspoken Divide

Growing up in Florida,
There was no segregation in schools.
Segregation had ended long ago.
But if you count the years, not that long ago.

At a young age, I was placed in ESL.
I looked Hispanic to them, so that was the label.
The school never read the records,
Not knowing I spoke perfect English.

I spent many months with the kindest teacher,
But everyone in that tiny class spoke Spanish.
I just wanted to go up to the school speaker,
And shout many things in English.

No one heard me.
They just looked at me,
But they did not see me.
I was placed by the color of my skin.

Segregated or not,
The atmosphere at schools screamed separation.
I was encouraged by teachers to join clubs in junior high.
Every club suggested was one my black peers would join.

The clubs' white peers were in,
The black peers were not there.
The black peers joined clubs too,
But the white peers were not there.

And where did that leave me,
The desi girl with long black hair?
She wore shalwar kameez and jeans only sometimes.
What on earth was she about?

I was placed based on my skin color once again.
I was too dark to join my white peers, but dark enough to
    join my black peers.
There was no in-between.
Who I thought I was did not matter in the system.

I was always accepted to join by black teachers when
    competing with my black friends.
There seemed to be concern from some teachers when
    competing in sports or any position.
Their concern was not from a place of dislike;
It was from a place of losing opportunities for black youth.

So much had already been taken from black people.
Who was this girl coming in and challenging opportunities
    for the black girls at school?
I understood this.
I took these experiences as a learning tool.

I was called down to the office many times.
A teacher or a student would always report me.
My dress or my nose ring made them uncomfortable.
My white peer next to me could have a nose ring, and it
    was fine.

This was not about my dress or the nose ring; it was the color of my skin.
I learned that back home in Pakistan or India; I was considered too dark.
The color of your skin determined beauty, which is absurd.
And here, it determined what your position was and what opportunities were allowed.

It took me a while to process the unfairness.
It took me a while to understand why,
Why people behaved the way they did.
It was a matter of privilege or loss.

Despite being placed by others growing up,
I never chose my friends by the color of their skin
But tried to stay in the company of kindness.
I never hid from the sun to avoid getting darker.
Nor did I ever use silly creams to be whiter.

What never changed was how comfortable I was in my own skin.
Society will make you think up many false reasons
Why the way you look is not good enough.
Do not let the thoughts produced by society shape your future.
Your skin, who you are, your identity are unique.
It's self-love, and it's beautiful.

Printed in the United States
by Baker & Taylor Publisher Services